AUSTRALIA'S UNIQUE
WILDLIFE

JIRI LOCHMAN

INTRODUCTION

Geographically, Australia is one of the most isolated land-masses on Earth and has been since its final split with Antarctica some 60 million years ago. Fortunately, this split occurred only after some unique quadrupeds — marsupials and monotremes — boarded Australia, via Antarctica, from South America. Only here in Australia were these two unorthodox groups of mammals given the opportunity to excel.

And excel they did. Australian marsupials were free to diversify, growing in all shapes and sizes up to the now extinct rhinoceros-size animals. They successfully occupied every possible niche of their new home and adopted every imaginable way of existence, from feeding on leaves, fruits and flower nectar high in the tree tops to tunneling deep underground in search of insect larvae and other inhabitants of the subterranean realms. They mastered a variety of ways of getting round from fast bipedal, hopping locomotion to bridging the distances between trees by gliding.

A red-necked Wallaby *Macropus Rufogriseus* with joey.

All of Australia's best loved animals — Kangaroos, Koalas, Wombats, Echidnas, Platypuses, Numbats, Quolls, Cuscuses, Possums, Marsupial Gliders, Tasmanian Devils, Potoroos, Bandicoots, Bilbies, Quokkas and Rock-wallabies — are the result of this experiment in evolution and none of them can be naturally found anywhere other than in Australia and a few neigbouring islands.

Except for Sea-lions and Fur-seals residing on offshore islands and frequenting the shores and river estuaries of Australia proper, the first non-flying placental mammals reached Australia some five million years ago. However, they were small, gentle, mousy-things which were not able to unsettle the by then well-established veteran Australian resident mammals. These rodents arrived in two waves and diversified here to over 60 species known as native mice and native rats.

Bats (some 70 species) and birds (about 10 times as many) had a far easier task in reaching Australian shores due to their ability to fly. Though without a doubt they are as fascinating, neither group is as exclusively Australian as are the marsupials. Still, about half of Australia's bat species are endemic and there are some bird families, like the Honeyeaters and Pardalotes, that are typically Australian.

The majority of Australian land reptiles and frogs are unique to Australia, too — some of their ancestors reached Australia even earlier than the marsupials. However, only one entire family, the Legless Lizards, can claim to be uniquely Australian, all the other families occur elsewhere.

Of course, the most numerous group of Australian fauna is the invertebrates. Beetles, butterflies, praying mantises, flies, cockroaches, termites, wasps, bees, ants, spiders, centipedes, snails and many others, all belong in this diverse and intriguing category, which is far from being completely known to science.

The last frontier of discovery for anyone interested in Australian wildlife lies beyond Australia's coasts, in its magnificent turquoise blue waters. Here, around the coral reefs, in underwater caves and among blades of seaweed, hide the myriad of colourful fishes and countless other organisms of all forms and shapes that baffle and astonish everyone who has the opportunity to witness them.

Opposite: Barrier Reef Anemonefish *Amphiprion akindynos* live among host anemones and are common along the Great Barrier Reef.

Opposite: The Western Pygmy-possum *Cercartetus concinnus* is a mouse-size nocturnal marsupial that feeds mainly on flower nectar and insects. It occurs in southern Australia between western Victoria and the west coast.

Above left: The two Western Pygmy-possums in this photograph are feeding on the nectar of a grevillea flower.

Above right: The Sugar Glider *Petaurus breviceps* is the most common of all Marsupial Gliders.

Above: The Rufous Ringtail Possum *Pseudocheirus peregrinus pulcher* is restricted to a small area of temperate rainforest around the Queensland–New South Wales border.

Right: Although primarily a tree dweller, the Mountain Brushtail Possum *Trichosurus caninus* spends plenty of time feeding on the ground.

Following pages: Eastern Grey Kangaroos *Macropus giganteus* are common in the eastern states where they can be easily observed in national park campsites.

Above: Eastern Grey Kangaroos are found in a variety of habitats, but prefer open woodlands.

Top: The Western Grey Kangaroo *Macropus fuliginosus* has a wide distribution ranging from south-western Australia to western Victoria and New South Wales to south-western Queensland.

Left: A Western Grey Kangaroo joey observes the world from the safety of its mother's pouch.

Above: The Black-footed Rock-wallaby *Petrogale lateralis* spends the daytime hidden in crevices, emerging at dusk to feed in the vicinity of its rocky habitat.

Right: The Black-footed Rock-wallaby is an expert rock climber which can negotiate near vertical rock faces with incredible ease.

Above: The Barrow Island Euro *Macropus robustus isabellinus* is restricted to Barrow Island off Western Australia.

Top: This rare photograph of a Euro in full flight was taken from a helicopter.

Left: The Euro *Macropus robustus* has the widest distribution of all kangaroos, occurring in all mainland states except Victoria and being equally at home in deserts, rocky ranges and forests.

Above: A familiar sight on Rottnest Island, the Quokka *Setonix brachyurus* is rare on the mainland.

Top: Gilbert's Potoroo *Potorous gilbertii* was presumed extinct before its rediscovery in 1994.

Right: The Red-necked Pademelon *Thylogale thetis* is a forest-dweller who feeds at night.

Above: The Sandy Inland Mouse *Pseudomys hermannsburgensis* inhabits much of the arid zone. It is seen here feeding on wattle seeds.

Above: The Spinifex Hopping-mouse *Notomys alexis* thoroughly checks the surroundings of its burrow before venturing out.

Mammals

Above: The Western False Pipistrelle *Falsistrellus mackenziei* is a small bat weighing between 15 and 25 grams. Its diet consists entirely of flying insects.

Right: A Bush Rat *Rattus fuscipes*, seen here feeding on Banksia flower nectar, is a native rodent.

Above: The Little Red Kaluta *Dasykaluta rosamondae* feeds mainly on large arthropods and small vertebrates. It had not been known to eat nectar before this photograph was taken.

Left: The Wongai Ningaui *Ningaui ridei*, despite its diminutive stature, is a ferocious hunter capable of subduing creatures its own size.

Above: The Numbat *Myrmecobius fasciatus* is a kitten-size termite eater and is one of only a few Australian mammals active during daytime hours.

Right: Juvenile Numbats cautiously explore near their home burrow before playing in the open.

Above: The Southern Brown Bandicoot *Isoodon obesulus* finds most of its food in the topsoil, using its long nose for locating and digging it out.

Above: The Western Barred Bandicoot *Perameles bougainville* is one of Australia's rarest mammals. It survives on only two offshore islands.

Opposite: A Golden Bandicoot *Isoodon auratus* approaches an egg-laying turtle to check whether the feast is ready.

Above: A unique photograph of the Golden Bandicoot devouring turtle eggs inside the egg chamber.

Above: The Southern Hairy-nosed Wombat *Lasiorhinus latifrons* is the only mammal confined to the Nullarbor Plain where lean years are far more frequent than abundant ones.

Right: The Common Wombat *Vombatus ursinus* occurs in high rainfall areas of temperate eastern Australia and Tasmania, and prefers native forests interspersed with grassy clearings.

Left: The Koala *Phascolarctos cinereus* is a browser, feeding exclusively on eucalyptus leaves. It spends most of the time in tree crowns, descending to the ground only to change trees.

Above left: After leaving the pouch, the baby Koala clings to its mother, riding on her back for five more months before it becomes fully independent.

Above right: Despite being reclusive and rather grumpy, the Koala would undoubtedly win a popularity contest of all Australian animals.

Following pages: The pups of the Dingo *Canis lupus dingo* are usually raised in an underground den, however in rocky terrain caves are often used.

Above: Dingoes usually have ginger-coloured pelts, however white individuals are frequent and, contrary to a common belief, are not a result of interbreeding with the domestic dog.

Right: The Dingo was originally from India. It was introduced to Australia some 4000 years ago.

Left and above: The Tasmanian Devil *Sarcophilus harrisii* is the largest surviving marsupial predator. The Tasmanian Devil occurs only in Tasmania, however it did live on the mainland until about 400 years ago. It is most common in eucalypt forests and coastal woodlands.

Above: The Northern Quoll *Dasyurus hallucatus* is the smallest and most common of all quolls.

Top: The Western Quoll *Dasyurus geoffroii* is one of the rarest marsupials.

Right: After nine weeks baby Western Quolls no longer fit into their mother's pouch.

Left: The Mulgara *Dasycercus cristicauda* is a nocturnal predator preying on a variety of small desert creatures. Depicted here is a mother with her offspring.

Above: The Greater Bilby *Macrotis lagotis*, in common with all other burrowing marsupials, has a rearwards opening pouch — an adaptation to protect joeys from the dirt.

Above: A female Australian Sea-lion *Neophoca cinerea* forms a firm bond with her cub.

Right: Despite their name, about 35 000 New Zealand Fur-seals *Arctocephalus forsteri* live on Australian offshore islands.

Following pages: Most Australian Sea-lion colonies are found on offshore islands.

Above: Australian Bottle-nosed Dolphins *Tursiops aduncas* are over a metre shorter than Bottle-nosed Dolphins in other parts of the world.

Left: The Humpback Whale *Megaptera novaeangliae* is a giant, weighing up to 29 tonnes. Yet it can leap out of the water with incredible dexterity.

Above and right: The Short-beaked Echidna *Tachyglossus aculeatus* is the only native mammal found in almost every habitat throughout Australia, including Tasmania.

Opposite and above: The Platypus *Ornithorhynchus anatinus* is seldom seen in the wild despite
being quite common east of the Great Dividing Range and in Tasmania. The Platypus seemed so bizarre
a creature that it was considered a hoax when the first specimens reached Europe.

Above: The male Australian King-Parrot *Alisterus scapularis*, with its prominent red coloured head, is much more conspicuous than the female.

Above: The Port Lincoln Parrot *Barnardius zonarius* is a common bird in Perth's city parks and is found throughout southern Western Australia.

Above left: The Long-billed Corella *Cacatua tenuirostris* requires tree hollows for nesting and has been severely affected by wholesale land clearing for agriculture.

Above right: Galahs *Cacatua roseicapilla* mark their tree when nesting, smearing themselves in the process and temporarily acquiring an untidy appearance.

Right: The Budgerigar *Melopsittacus undulatus* has become a popular cage bird throughout the world.

Above left: The Rainbow Lorikeet *Trichoglossus haematodus* occurs naturally in wooded areas of the eastern states and Tasmania, and it was introduced to Western Australia.

Above right: The Major Mitchell's Cockatoo, or Pink Cockatoo, *Cacatua leadbeateri* is an exceptionally handsome parrot. It is confined to the dry areas of the southern half of Australia.

Left: The Red-tailed Black Cockatoo *Calyptorhynchus banksii* is one of the largest Australian parrots. It is rare in captivity and therefore very attractive to poachers.

Following pages: Galahs gather by a waterhole — like all other seed-eating birds they depend on the availability of fresh water.

Above: The Little Penguin *Eudyptula minor* is the only penguin to call Australia home.

Top: The Pied Cormorant *Phalacrocorax varius* is a common sight around the Australian coast.

Right: The Australian Pelican *Pelecanus conspicillatus* is Australia's largest flying bird.

Above: The Red-capped Dotterel *Charadrius ruficapillus* is a ground-nesting bird which simulates injury when disturbed, dragging its wings on the ground and luring intruders away from its nest.

Opposite: The Black-fronted Dotterel *Charadrius melanops* has expanded its range to New Zealand, where it was unkown until 1954.

Above: The Caspian Tern *Hydroprogne caspia* is the largest of all Australian terns and can be easily identified by its conspicuous red bill.

Opposite: The Pied Oystercatcher *Haematopus ostralegus* is present on beaches and tidal flats all around Australia and is especially common in Tasmania.

Above: Despite its large size the Brolga *Grus rubicunda* usually remains unnoticed until it takes off with an accompanying loud honking sound.

Left: The wetlands of tropical Australia are teeming with birdlife like Pied Geese, Australian Pelicans and Brolgas.

Following pages: The Large Egret *Egretta alba* uses its bill like a spear, darting at any unsuspecting prey that comes within its reach.

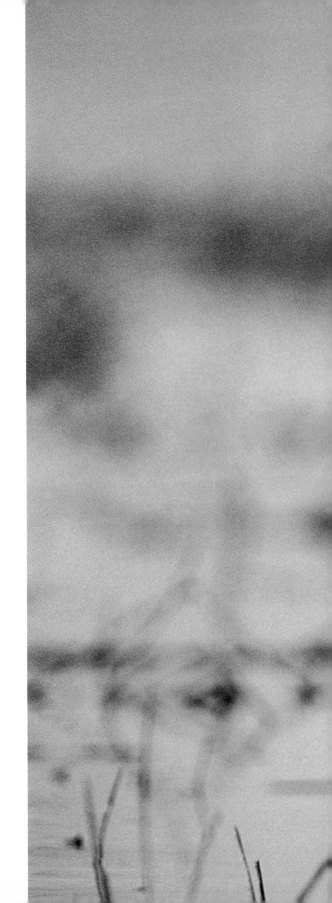

Above: The Black-necked Stork, or Jabiru, *Ephippiorhynchus asiaticus* is Australia's only stork. The female, shown here, is recognisable by her yellow eyes — males' eyes are black.

Right: The White-faced Heron *Ardea novaehollandiae* is the most commonly encountered of all Australian herons and egrets, occurring in wetlands, rivers, lakes and oceans.

Above: The Coot *Fulica atra* thrives in many metropolitan parks with established lakes.

Top: An Australasian Little Grebe *Tachybaptus novaehollandiae* chick waits for its parent who forages for food underwater.

Left: The Great Crested Grebe *Podiceps cristatus* builds a floating nest made of water plants on which both parents incubate the eggs.

Above and right: The Black Swan *Cygnus atratus* is a famous Australian oddity — its colour is in sharp contrast with that of white swans of other continents. Black Swans fiercely defend their cygnets against other swans and intruders daring to come too close.

"BILYANA"

Above: The Wedge-tailed Eagle *Aquila audax* with its wingspan of up to 2.5 metres is the largest Australian bird of prey.

Left: The White-breasted Sea-eagle *Haliaeetus leucogaster* favours building its huge nest of sticks on a cliff or similarly inaccessible place.

Above: The Brown Falcon *Falco berigora* is seen here devouring a Monitor Lizard. Reptiles form a large part of the Brown Falcon's diet.

Above: The Peregrine Falcon *Falco peregrinus* is the fastest bird in the world, capable of reaching phenomenal speeds of 140 kilometres an hour.

Above left: The Laughing Kookaburra *Dacelo novaeguineae* is the largest kingfisher in the world. It is best known for the strange territorial cackle that gave it its common name.

Above right: The Tawny Frogmouth *Podargus strigoides* is a nocturnal bird that feeds on a variety of insects and other small creatures.

Right: The Boobook Owl *Ninox novaehollandiae* is the smallest and the most common of all Australian owls. It is named after the sound of its call — 'boobook'.

Following pages: The Emu *Dromaius novaehollandiae* is a large flightless bird endemic to Australia. When chased it can run at speeds of 50 kilometres per hour.

Above: The bower of the Spotted Bowerbird *Chlamydera maculata* is a solid structure built of carefully selected and arranged sticks, and adorned mainly by white objects.

Top: The Regent Bowerbird *Sericulus chrysocephalus* inhabits temperate rainforests of south-eastern Queensland and north-eastern New South Wales.

Left: The Spotted Bowerbird male spends most of his time tending his bower. This species is the only bowerbird found in the arid inland of Australia.

Above: The Yellow-throated Miner *Manorina flavigula* is the only miner found in the deserts and the western half of Australia.

Above: The Singing Honeyeater *Lichenostomus virescens* has the widest distribution of all honeyeaters.

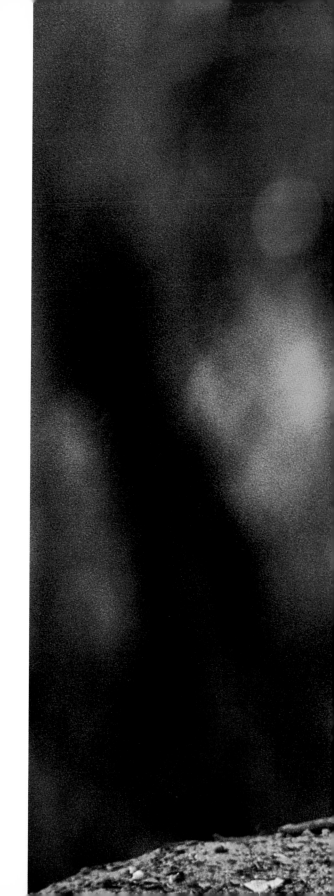

Above: The Diamond Dove *Geopelia cuneata* gets its name from the white spots — or diamonds — on its wings. This pair is taking part in a nuptial display.

Top: The Spinifex Pigeon *Geophaps plumifera* occurs in two distinct subspecies. Depicted is the white-bellied form from the Kimberley and central deserts.

Right: The Mallee Fowl *Leipoa ocellata* incubates its eggs by harnessing the heat from decomposing leaves.

Above: The Soft Knob-tailed Gecko *Nephrurus levis* lives in the deserts of central and western Australia.

Opposite: The Soft Knob-tailed Gecko *Nephrurus laevissimus* is a small nocturnal lizard
that spends the day in a burrow in the sand.

Above: The Thorny Devil *Moloch horridus* is a slow-moving, 10-centimetre long, harmless lizard. Its only defence is its strange armour of spines.

Right: The Frill-necked Lizard *Chlamydosaurus kingii* takes its name from the large frill around its neck, which it spreads to frighten off any aggressors.

Above: Crossing the territory of another Perentie *Varanus giganteus* is a risky business.

Top: The Perentie is the largest Australian lizard, growing to two metres in length. It is big enough to swallow a small wallaby.

Left: The Bungarra *Varanus panoptes* is slightly smaller than the Perentie. It feeds on a variety of creatures, both invertebrates and vertebrates.

Above: The Monk Snake *Rhinoplocephalus monachus* hunts at night for small lizards. Its most distinctive characteristic is the black-coloured top of its head.

Opposite: The Australian Bronzeback *Dendrelaphis punctulatus* is a non-venomous, diurnal snake that can be encountered near water, where it hunts for frogs.

Following pages: The Freshwater Crocodile *Crocodylus johnstoni* inhabits rivers, lakes and swamps of tropical Australia — fish, frogs and birds are its main diet.

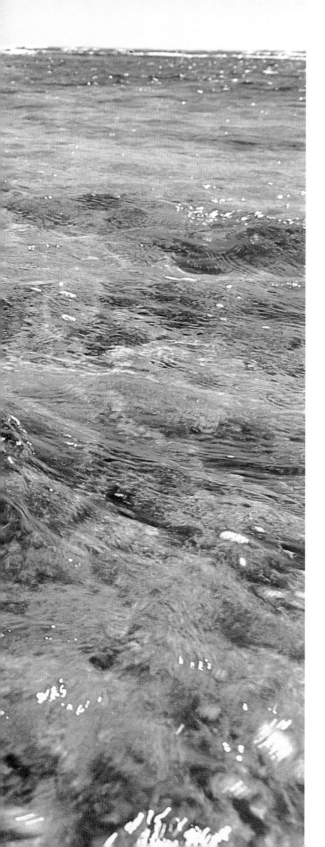

Above: Once seen, the Pig-nosed Turtle *Carettochelys insculpta* cannot be mistaken for any other turtle. It has a proboscis-like nose with prominent nostrils.

Top: An adult Green Turtle *Chelonia mydas* is herbivorous and weighs up to 130 kilograms, while juveniles, such as the one pictured, are meat eaters.

Left: This Green Turtle is returning to the ocean after the exhausting activity of egg laying. The sea turtles are extremely unwieldy on land.

Above: The Waterholding Frog *Cyclorana platycephala* is well adapted for life in deserts.

Top: Main's Frog *Cyclorana maini* lives in central Western Australia and the Northern Territory.

Right: Spencer's Burrowing Frog *Limnodynastes spenceri* survives drought by staying buried in the riverbed sand. It resurfaces after the rain to breed in waterpools.

Above: The Brown Tree Frog *Litoria ewingii* inhabits creeks, swamps and waterholes of Tasmania, Victoria, southern New South Wales and south-eastern South Australia.

Left: The Bull Frog *Litoria moorei* is popularly known as the 'Motorcycle Frog' because of its call resembling a motorcycle revving up.

Above: Because of their brilliant colours Jewel Beetles were ruthlessly collected in the past. This Jewel Beetle *Castiarina vegeta* is feeding on a tea-tree.

Above: A Jewel Beetle *Stigmodera gratiosa* feeding on a featherflower. Jewel Beetles have now been declared protected fauna.

Above: After every meal a Praying Mantis *Orthodera* sp. will carefully clean its raptorial forelegs, organs used mainly for catching and holding prey.

Left: This nymph Praying Mantis *Hierodula* sp. carries its thorny forelegs in the typical prayer-like fashion that gave rise to the name of the group.

Above: Caterpillars, such as the Hawk Moth Caterpillar *Psilogramma sp.*, are the larvae of butterflies and moths, of which there are over 20 000 recognised species living in Australia.

Right: The Birdwing Butterfly *Ornithoptera priamus* is the largest Australian butterfly, occuring in lowland rainforests of northern Queensland. Depicted is the bigger sex — female.

Above left: By inflating itself and erecting long, sharp spines the Porcupinefish *Diodon nicthemerus* becomes an unwieldy morsel no sane predator dares to swallow.

Above right: The Harlequin Fish *Othos dentex* is an inquisitive fish, often accompanied by a Western Cleaner Clingfish *Cochleoceps bicolor,* seen here on its face.

Left: The Purple-tailed Sea Jelly *Pseudorhiza haeckei* is one of the most common sea jellies. It can be encountered along Australia's western and southern coasts.

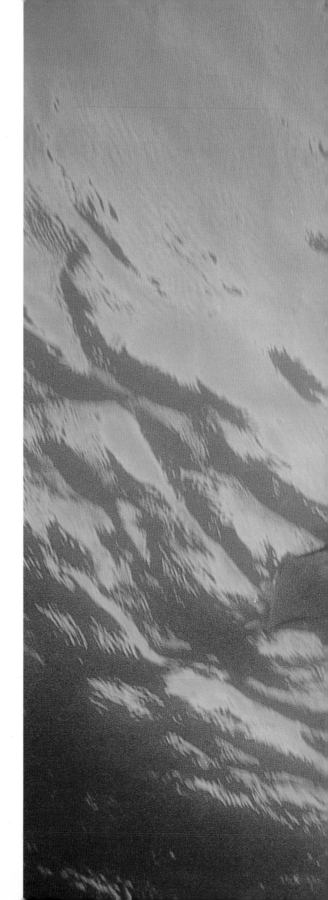

Above: The White-tipped Reef Shark *Triaenodon obesus*, though usually non-aggressive, should nevertheless be approached with caution.

Right: A Manta Ray *Manta birostris* is an unforgettable sight. Like most oceanic giants, it feeds on plankton and is therefore totally harmless.